MW00426681

This book belongs to:

____

Made in United States
North Haven, CT
24 November 2021

11469597R00061